A Light in the Darkness

A Light in the Darkness

PEGGY ROWAN

RESOURCE *Publications* • Eugene, Oregon

Resource Publications
An Imprint of Wipf and Stock Publishers
199 W. 8th Ave., Suite 3
Eugene, OR 97401

www.wipfandstock.com

PAPERBACK ISBN: 978-1-6667-4685-3
HARDCOVER ISBN: 978-1-6667-4686-0
EBOOK ISBN: 978-1-6667-4687-7

VERSION NUMBER 072022

To all the prodigals out there,
may you find your way home.

Lord, you light my lamp;
my God illuminates my darkness.

—Ps 18:28 CSB

Contents

Acknowledgements

My parents who have long passed over the veil,
for showing me how to follow Jesus.

My sisters, Patty Dunn and Penny Wampler,
who never stopped praying.

Stephen Hayes, because you teared up every time
you said Jesus' name.

David Meece, for unknowingly going on walks with me;
may I always light a candle in the rain.

But mostly, Jesus, for taking me back with open arms.
I am completely undone by his love.

Introduction

BACK IN 1989 AT the ripe old age of fifteen, I wrote the song lyrics below. My sisters and I got up in church and I sang these words with all my might. Less than five years later I began a prodigal journey that would last over two decades before I found my way back home again.

Upon my return, I wondered if I would ever share my story with others who may have turned away from God. If perhaps, through my words, they would turn back around and realize that Jesus is always the best decision we can make. If you are straddling the fence, I hope the story that follows will convince you to choose Jesus. I hope that this intimate book you hold in your hands (or see on your screen) is me being a light in the darkness which might surround you.

A Light in the Darkness

I wanna be a light in the darkness
I wanna show the world Jesus is the one.
I wanna show the world there is a better way
And I won't stop until my work is done.
I want my light to shine forever
Always brighter than the sun
I wanna take the world to heaven
And introduce them to God's only son.
I wanna show the world to Jesus
I wanna show them Jesus in me
I wanna shine in a world so dark
Shine so bright, they can't help but see.

1

Dusk

You are all children of the light and children of the day.
We do not belong to the night or to the darkness.

—*1 Thess 5:5 NIV*

SHE IS PIOUS IN clothes that cover most of her skin. Makeup is vanity, and vanity is a sin. Selfless in her acts, she asks for and takes nothing. She is on earth strictly for the benefit of others. She says to me; "keep your eyes on Jesus", but I won't listen. She may be happy with her life choices, but I am not her. I long for a life of freedom and independence. I long for a life of my own.

Bright lights brush over a crowded room as I move to the beat drenched in sweat. I will regret this in the morning, but for now I am in a hypnotic state swaying to the music. The DJ is playing top forty, and the alcohol is making me feel as if I am shimmering from head to toe. I feel like I am floating in a sea of people. My friends are around me . . . a good-looking guy starts to approach. Here in this dark place, life is beautiful.

Another love dissolves, I have been here before. "You don't need me" he said, and I know he's right, but I want him . . . still. The heart inside my chest will shut down, bitterness will build a cage I will lock myself up in. God is love and love has forsaken me.

2

There's a Fly in the Casserole

Elijah went before the people and said, "How long will you waver between two opinions? If the LORD is God, follow him; but if Baal is God, follow him." But the people said nothing.

—*1 Kgs 18:21 NIV*

I WATCH AS A fly descends on the casserole, landing lightly on the corn flake topping. The banana pudding is beginning to erode. The pies on the dessert table remain stable, for now. It is another Sunday afternoon in summer, and I am sitting at a picnic table outside of a small church. My parents are mingling with other parishioners. Service has just ended, and my butt is sore from sitting on a hard wooden pew. I am sweating and the paper fans showing Jesus holding a lamb are of no use. The long-winded preacher had warned us of the dangers of sin and a lake of fire. When it finally comes time to eat, I go for the KFC bucket suspicious of the other dishes just as I am suspicious about what the preacher has just told us.

The small white church still sits at the end of a street tucked away in a southside neighborhood. On Easter, we hunt colorful eggs to put in pink-ribboned baskets. We dressed in white shiny shoes, white tights, and new pastel dresses. On Christmas, we stood on the stage with towels on our heads repeating the lines we had spent months trying to memorize. I can still smell the musty scent of the basement where I first learned about Jesus, can taste the tart grape juice and stale slither of bread, can hear the red-faced preacher screaming about a lake of fire. I can see all the men sitting on the front row where women were not allowed.

I am seated beside my mother when I hear a high-pitched scream come out of her. She is not prone to public outburst, embarrassed, I slide further down into my seat. I start sitting in the corner next to a window as if I can escape outside. What overcomes her that she can't contain within herself? My mother participates in the Ladies Auxiliary, sings in the choir, and volunteers to clean the church. My father sits at the end of the pew yelling "amen, brother" at the preacher. He passes the silver offering plate, plays his Gibson for anyone who asks, and helps keep the grounds and build whatever needs building. My sisters and I follow along as if it's the most natural thing in the world. We'd stand beside our mother on a bridge to watch baptisms in the river below, skirts blowing up as the car whiz by. This is the path we are on, and we are not to stray from it.

I straddle the fence my sisters jump over. I hold back during the altar calls, gripping the back of the pew in front of me. I'm unsure about this Christian life. There are so many rules, and I refuse to serve a God who considers women less important than men.

I feel my heart like a hammer in my chest during "Just as I am". I feel goosebumps on my skin during some of the worship songs — imagine a God who is all powerful and yet still cares about each one of us. But I don't want my life planned out in front of me; get saved, get married, have kids, live a life full of tent revivals and Billy Graham. I want to break free from this old-time religion and do life my way.

The 80s usher in a new wave of Christian music. DC Talk is proud to be Jesus Freaks, Carmen has us cheering on The Champion, and bands like Petra and Stryper are rockin' their way into our Walkman. It is also the age of the "Left Behind" series which leaves us both heartbroken and terrified. I'm not allowed to go to movies, parties, or school events. I *am* allowed to travel with a local Christian band, go to concerts with the youth group, and hold hands with the boys from church.

A few of us in the youth group haven't walked down to the altar yet. Being a Christian doesn't sound like fun, sin sounds much more enticing. At home, I am an outcast. I'm going to be the one who will be left behind and break the family circle in that "sweet by and by". Worrying my family weighs heavy on me. The youth group leader pulls me to the side and tells me: "if you go, the others will go."

It's a Sunday morning when I finally let go of the pew in front of me. I walk up to the altar just as I am. Men are bowed around me murmuring something I don't understand. Are they asking God to forgive all my preteen sins?? Isn't this between me and God? I don't say anything, but tears are falling down my face. Was I feeling guilty or do the people around me make me feel this way? I get up feeling light-headed and see the huge smile on my father's face. True to what the youth group pastor told me; the other fence-straddlers go to the altar the following Sunday.

The next day, I go to school. Life remains the same around me even though I have been "born again". I am full of teenage angst. I'm bored, restless, and angry. There are too many questions that I am not supposed to ask, so I don't. I'm supposed to read the Bible and accept every word even if I don't understand it. I'm supposed to testify during service but hate the thought of standing up blubbering in front of everyone. I have written some songs that my sisters and I get up and sing in church. I sense God in the lyrics and a spiritual connection to him when we sing. But there are feelings and questions that continue to gnaw at me; why am I "less than" because I'm a woman? Why am I supposed to fight what I am feeling? Why do I desire to do all the things the church is telling me is sin? I pretend to believe even as confusion and rebellion eat away at me. The older I get, the more forced church is becoming for me;

songs I can no longer stand to sing, feet I hate to wash, silence that I can no longer hold.

I am like that fly in the casserole—I don't belong here.

My thoughts were full of other things when I wandered off the path.

—*Dante Alighieri,* Inferno

3

Drawn to the Darkness

Everyone who does evil hates the light and will not come into
the light for fear that their deeds will be exposed.

—*John 3:20 NIV*

BEAUTIFULLY CREEPY MUSIC PLAYS softly overhead as I turn a dark corner expecting a clown or someone with a chainsaw to jump out at me. Instead, I find myself walking through hanging bags of body parts. They sway as I walk through looking straight ahead to the black curtains that will lead to another scene. Then out of the shadows steps a child, face painted white with dark circles around their eyes, long clumpy black hair covering most of their face. They approach in a white flowing gown that gives the impression that they are levitating. Out of their mouth comes an inhuman sound. It is like walking through a nightmare.

I scan the wares of creepy dolls, spiderwebbed bookshelves, and blood splattered mirrors. I'm not here for the workshops, I don't actually work in the haunted attractions industry—I am here for the haunts. I ride in a bus among friends to various award-winning haunted attractions throughout the Midwest and East

Coast. As my friend and I are walking to the ballroom of the hotel, she tells me that her and her husband are atheist. Without missing a beat, I tell her I'm one too. As soon as the words are out of my mouth, I feel my heart twist. I denied God existed. I had lied. I pull the mask down over my face so she can't see the guilt and shame. I walk into the costume ball and blend in with the other demons and monsters.

I have long since lost my desire to be chased with a bladeless chainsaw in the dark and now feed my love for Halloween by writing horror stories. What attracted me to those dark places? They allowed me to sink into the shadows. Walking through haunted attractions was a way to conquer my everyday fears—because the man with the chainsaw never caught me.

I am in Lily Dale, New York sitting on a screened in porch across from a medium. Lily Dale is a small spiritual community with full vibrant gardens, colored cottages, and fairy trails. After a few moments of studying my face and the tarot cards in front of her, she says; "You've lost your laughter, you have to get it back."

I have consulted mediums throughout my early adult life searching for a way to unveil the mystery of the spiritual realm. I acquired a small collection of tarot cards in hopes of reading my own future. I purchased a Ouija board hoping to conjure up someone from the spirit world to provide me with the answers I was looking for. Oh, the irony.

Shortly after leaving church for good, I started to explore other religions and spirituality. I read books about sorcery and magic and go to seances to conjure up spirits. I stand in a circle of witches calling out to the four directions. Witchcraft was so enticing with its casting of spells, ability to control something or someone—but that's Hollywood witches. These witches in my circle revere the earth, practice aromatherapy, and study herbology. They do not however, practice the "dark arts".

The paint is peeling from the walls of the Trans-Allegheny Asylum in West Virginia. The tour guide lays a lit flashlight down on a table to see if a spiritual entity will make it go out. I have a sensation in my chest, a kind of heavy oppression as if some horrible acts occurred here in the not-so-distant past.

I walk through the graffitied remnants of long-dead criminals at the Mansfield State Reformatory. A friend and I walk around holding an EVP device, calling out "is anyone here?" All is silent with the exception of the fast-paced fluttering of bat wings as they fly overhead.

A soiled teddy bear sits in a stilled swing. We are in an abandoned amusement park which has become overtaken by the wild. We listen to the tales of Lake Shawnee's dark history. I walk around the small lake and linger beside the moss-filled seats of a Ferris wheel, it's quite here but ominous. We leave disheartened that we didn't encounter anyone from across the veil or hear the echo of ghostly cries from a child.

My ghost comes to me in a room at the Hyatt Regency in Buffalo. My cousin and I are on a trip to visit Niagara Falls. It's around 3a.m and I wake to see a man kneeling beside my bed. He is a solid figure with tightly curled white hair peeking out from beneath an old-fashioned bellhop cap. His jacket is red with gold buttons and trimming. His eyes are a luminescent blue and he appears to be soundlessly laughing at me. I think he is a dream; I blink rapidly but he remains there. I call out for my cousin, but she is deep in sleep and doesn't stir. Eventually he fades from my view. It's easy to explain away a lot of instances, but I have always felt vulnerable to spiritual entities. I had spent the early part of my adult life inviting them in.

I am an angry young woman. Angry at what I am told is to be my life. Get married, have kids, continue coming to this church, and smile as if I am happy to be here. I search for a place to quell this anger and find a women's organization that fights for equality. This organizations tells me I am as important as a man. I have found a place I belong.

We are hosting a weekend conference in downtown Columbus. As we march down High Street holding signs, I spot a small group of protestors. In their midst is a thin man dressed as if he stepped out of a 50's sitcom. He is yelling into a megaphone;

"Sinners, you will burn in hell!" A pious looking woman stands beside him holding a sign which reads "I submit to my husband." The women marching beside me start yelling back: "Sexist, racist, anti-gay! Born again bigot go away!" We march on as a battle began to stir within me. I become overwhelmed with guilt. It feels as if I am disrespecting my parents. It's true that I don't want to live the kind of Christian life my family is, but I also don't want to be on the complete opposite side of them. After the march comes to an end, I leave and don't go back to the conference.

Throughout my entire life I find other organizations and ways to support women. This is a priority. If you are a woman who was taught that you are not as important as a man, I encourage you to talk it over with Jesus. I did. In the clearest of ways and with no hesitation, a small voice whispered; "if you had been the only person on earth, I still would've gone to the cross to save you."

This essay is intended to talk about my personal experience and not to place judgement on various women's groups, the Haunted Attraction industry, or any religious organizations.

My head is swimming in a blur,
Uneasiness about my walking,
I want to fall and go into a deep sleep.
I know what awaits me in the morning.
Knowing I shouldn't get in the car,
I regain soberness for a few minutes
because I need to think clearly.
I need to make it home and stop for food.
A cloudy mind trying to remember.
An ache—dull and lasting.
Stomach churning, do I let the liquid come out?
Can I lay here and sleep through the day?
I'm bent over staring at the inside of a toilet bowl.
Regret fills my mind, why do I do this
weekend after weekend
when I tell myself I won't ever do this again?
Is it worth that feeling of . . .
what is that feeling anyway?
Numbness from everything.
Do I hurt inside? No.
Do I care about anything? No.
Am I having a good time and relaxing? Yes.
Is there a better way to feel this?

4

What the Locust Ate

Woe to those who call evil good and good evil, who put darkness for light and light for darkness, who put bitter for sweet and sweet for bitter.

—Isa 5:20 NIV

IT'S A TUESDAY NIGHT and I slide onto a ragged red barstool. Cigarette smoke lingers in the atmosphere, a ban won't clean the air for a few more years. Familiar faces are seated around a polished wooden bar, they turn toward the door every time it opens. "Sweet Home Alabama" is coming out of a juke box from a small area which doubles as a dance floor on Friday and Saturday nights. After placing my bottle of Bud Light on the bar, the bartender walks around to give me a hug. If the guys from Grainger are there, I will join their table. If not, I will sit here next to a guy with fishhooks in his cap, we call him "Big Dog." Either way, I am home.

They became my second family, making all the bad times in my life less painful. They made all the good times more memorable. I will forever think of that place and those people with a smile on my face.

I didn't depend on alcohol, but I enjoyed it immensely. I fondly remember drinking and dancing on the weekends, sharing my workday in a bar, a better option than going home to be by myself, spending a Sunday afternoon watching football or basketball from a barstool. I love a good party and the taste of a cold beer on the first warm day of Spring. The moment you get too tipsy before you plunge over to being drunk, *that* moment is exquisite. I always longed to stay in those moments where nothing mattered. I never could though, I always spilled over. I stayed too long and drunk too much trying to make that warm, fuzzy feeling last.

I shouldn't have been driving that night and looking back nothing has convinced me more that God had his hand over me. I ordered a Long Island Iced Tea to ease the workday away. Then a regular would come in; "I got the next round." Then another regular and another round. It's alright, I thought, home is only two turns away. A stranger told me the story, about how he had followed me as I swerved in front of him. How I almost hit another car head on. He followed me as I took the turn into my apartment complex too quickly, too sharply, and ran into the metal gate surrounding the pool. The gate gave a little but kept me from driving into the pool. I crawled out of my car and onto the ground as this blond-haired stranger stood looking down on me asking; "do you know how lucky you are?"

Two short years out of high school, I walk down the aisle as a bride. Marriage was my way out of the Christian home I was suffocating in. Two short years after that, we drive over to his friend's house where he gets out of the car and walks away from our marriage. His face wears a look of questioning apprehension, he is wondering if he will regret this decision (he would). I have that same feeling when I walk away from God. I didn't want salvation now, but I might want it later. I might be making a mistake, and I'm not sure what this mistake will eventually cost me.

A few weeks after my husband leaves me, I become involved with someone and for the next twenty years men would walk in and out of my life. None of my relationships lasted longer than a few years. When I was by myself, I focused on my career, writing, and having fun. When I was with someone, he became my sole focus. I thought this was how it was supposed to be. I loved the feeling of falling in love but became restless and bored quite easily. One relationship would spiral to the cusp of violence and by the time I reach forty I have nothing to show for love except a past full of mental abuse and heartache.

The tiara on top of the Great America Tower comes into view and reveals the spectacular Cincinnati skyline. Welcome to your new home, I tell myself. It's March 2013 and my employer has opened a new office and moved me down here from Columbus. I jumped at the chance to start a new life and shrug off my past. Unbeknownst at the time, the move would catapult my career. I become a part of the office leadership, move into a management role, and obtain a six-figure salary. Career-wise, I am at the top of my game. I spend the first few months making new friends, exploring new places, and attending new events. Then one of those new friends sends me on another spiral. He constantly talks to me about God and church, until the evening we are out drinking, and he asks me to go home with him while his wife is away. I say "no", I am too old to make these kinds of bad decisions again. But the offer stings and brings all the bad relationship bitterness back to the surface to seethe underneath my skin. The idea of a new life gets diminished, the tiara falls.

My anger against God reemerges and the past I thought I left behind comes roaring back. I become hard, left sour by broken dreams and the expectations I have for love. I smile at the world hiding behind a façade. My heart dissolves to ashes, my bones become dry. I've spent years looking for a knight in shining armor when the entire time a King was standing in front of me with open arms.

5

From Prodigal to Peace

So, he got up and went to his father.
But while he was still a long way off,
his father saw him and was filled with compassion for him;
he ran to his son, threw his arms around him, and kissed him.

—*Luke 15:20 NIV*

THE MEMORY OF MY walk to the altar is vague, time has diminished it. The return is still fresh in my mind. It's a sunny October morning. Across from the motionless roller coasters of Kings Island sits a church called Rivers Crossing. I hadn't stepped foot inside a church in almost twenty years and I consider turning around and going back home. My Sunday routine is a peaceful one. The sun reflects off the lake behind my apartment causing a shimmering effect on my ceiling. I eat breakfast while watching the latest episode of Mysteries at the Museum, then I dive into a good book with no demands on my time. This particular Sunday morning I am searching for something that the past two decades have stolen from me.

This is not the church I grew up in. The "pews" are in the style of a movie theatre. There are no hymn books. The room is dark until bright lights hit the stage and a worship band begins. The words aren't familiar to me. I'm sitting in a seat in the last row hoping no one sits down next to me. I want to avoid talking to anyone. I look behind me and see four people in blue welcome shirts standing between me and the door, there is no escaping God's wrath if he chooses to rain it down upon me.

I live like a celebrity, at least that's what my friends tell me. I travel to Europe, go on frequent cruises, I have a big job title and the big salary to go along with it. I have hit my forties and there is no bad relationship to get out of, no addition to overcome, no recent tragedies. But there is a side of me my friends can't see. I have searched in a bottle, in relationships, in my career, and yet peace continues to elude me. I am like a piece of driftwood tossing about in ocean waves. I search for peace even as the Prince of Peace has come looking for me.

As we step off the plane at DFW, I am hit with a blast of abundant sunshine. It is like stepping into a warm hug. My colleagues and I are here to make a business pitch for a multi-million-dollar project. I have been so anxious about this pitch I had asked my sisters to pray about it. I fumble my way through and in the end, we win the project. It's one of the highlights of my career. I start working with their marketing manager who happens to be tall, attractive, and about a decade younger than me. As always, God knows how to get my attention. There is something else I notice about him though; he has an aura of peace. No matter what is going on he is forever calm. I imagine it's his youthfulness, that life has yet to leave him jaded. We quickly become friends and as I scroll his Facebook page reading scripture after scripture in his posts.

I sit in that back row of Rivers Crossing listening to the worship team. I am awaiting a knock on my heart and find myself getting anxious. I don't feel the invitation I felt those many years ago. Perhaps I have strayed too far, my heart has become too hard, my denial of his existence too blasphemous. I had heard once that there was a place you could get to where you would be too far away for him to reach—you would be cut off from him forever.

The pastor gets up, he is about my age and his reference to the eighties makes him relatable. He holds my attention. He is talking about ways we can rediscover our purpose. As he talks, my heart begins to beat wildly. I begin to sense a change and a rush of peace flows through me as if the wind itself has gotten underneath my skin. Instead of the knock I was expecting, I sense arms spread wide in front of me. "If you want to come back to me, surrender your life. I still love you and I have been waiting for you." He has left the ninety-nine to come find me. In this church called Rivers Crossing, I cross the river back to God and I walk out squinting at the sun.

6

Shouts in the Desert

The night is almost gone, and the day is near.
Therefore, let us lay aside the deeds of darkness
and put on the armor of light.

—*Rom 13:12 NASB*

I AM SITTING ON the stairs of my apartment in Dallas. I am on a call fumbling out an excuse of why I can't go to an interview with the hiring agency on the other end. There is no real excuse, in fact, I should go. I am still waiting for a job here in Dallas and my funds are dwindling. The hiring agency would most likely be able to find me a job quickly. But my heart is hammering inside my chest, a loud indication from God that I shouldn't go. Why wouldn't God want me to find a successful job here? It would be illogical for me not to go to this interview, but I am certain it is God making my heart pound. I hang up the phone without further explanation.

I've just gotten home from the Flourish conference at Covenant church. It's the first Christian conference I have attended. I feel reignited, I feel blessed, I feel my cup overflowing. The church is right down the road from my apartment. From the moment I walked in, I knew I was home. It was a larger church than I was used to, but everyone was welcoming. Stephen Hayes was the pastor and there was something I instantly noticed about him—his eyes would well up every time he said the name of Jesus. I want to be like that, I think. I want to love Jesus SO much that I am moved to tears at the mention of his name.

It's the day after Christmas 2016 and I stare star-struck at the sheer size of AT&T stadium. I am here to watch my two favorite teams: the Cowboys and the Lions. I am spending the week in Dallas having escaped the snow and cold back home. While in Dallas, I take in a puppet show at Geppetto's Theatre and get a taste of being a kid again as fake snowflakes fall over me like confetti. I go to the Gaylord Texan Resort and experience a Christmas wonderland. I cap off my holiday season with a NYE party at a gothic style mansion called Old Red Museum. On a "Hidden Dallas" tour I stroll through a sculpture garden with gargoyles at its gate. Contained within this secret garden are dragons with serpent shaped bodies and an angel blowing on a trumpet. I have stumbled into a fairytale. I have stumbled into a city full of life.

During my holiday in Dallas, I have several conversations with God regarding the current state of my life. I want a new purpose and to get out of the same pattern of broken relationships and loneliness. I ask God to change the life I have spent so many years creating. I tour a couple of apartments dreaming of a new life. By the end of January 2017, I have a plan. I will leave it all behind; my twenty-year career, my six-figure salary, all my friends . . . my drive for success. I am going to go somewhere where I have only a couple of acquaintances. I am moving to a city I have only visited twice.

I had filled out an application to one of the apartments and had gotten notification of approval. I found a marketing firm and had applied; they ask me to fly in for an interview on Valentine's Day. The director and I connect right away, and the interview goes well. I get done earlier than expected and go back to the airport to mill around until my flight. I am having lunch at a Chili's when the hostess and I start chatting. He mentions a book by CS Lewis and then he mentions Jesus. Something must have lit-up in my eyes, because he says; "Oh, I see you know him to." I am so elated; my friend Jesus keeps popping up everywhere.

Thinking everything was in order I give my notice, letting go of the only thing that had stayed consistent my entire adult life. It doesn't come without hesitation. To my friends and colleagues, it might have seemed illogical to move without knowing what I was going to do. But I have decided that I am going to trust God to provide whatever I need. I had money in the bank but I was still taking a financial risk. I'm reminded of when Elijah was at Cherith, how God commanded the ravens to feed him there. God had made sure Elijah was sustained during that time—He would do the same for me.

A job offer doesn't come before I leave, but I have been assured that there will be a position for me when I get there. Moving day comes and I say goodbye to my home of the past four years. I will miss my friends from work, my church, and the way the pond behind me shimmers on the ceiling. I follow the moving truck down and we stop in Nashville to spend the night. The next morning torrential rain is pouring down over Memphis. It's not long before I realize I have run off the road and am driving on the grass. If a guardrail would have been there, I would have damaged my car or worse. I straighten out as a semi-truck hovers near by until I find my way back on to the road safely. I am not alone in my travels.

My apartment is on the north side of Dallas in Addison. The first night I lay awake in shock. I can't believe I have left my career behind; it had been my security blanket for twenty years. I have no one to talk to but God. Over the next few days, I learn that the position I was promised isn't going to pan out. While I wait for another to open, I enjoy the sunny, stretched out days. There is a small park next to my apartment building. Upon turning the corner to the park, the first sight that comes into view is a burst of color from the Crape Myrtle trees. Trinity Christian Academy sits on one side and Bent Tree Child Center on the other. The park has literature quotes on a stone walkway leading up to a grove of trees.

I start taking daily walks in the park. I find comfort in the sounds of the children at play, they wave at me as I walk by. I seemed to have forgotten everything about being a Christian. I don't even know how to talk to Jesus anymore. I start reciting Psalms 23 out loud walking around in the shadows of the trees. Dallas would become the green pastures that God has led me to. I picture Jesus sitting beside me on one of the park benches listening to me rattle on. This was how I learn how to pray again. I lament about my job situation. I don't really want to go back to working in an office day after day, but I know I have to. It's the only way I would survive here. I feel vulnerable without a job, as if I'm walking on a suspended rope bridge peering down into a rocky canyon below. Unlike back in Ohio, my family isn't nearby for me to run to. I only have Jesus, but he will be enough.

When I am not taking walks with Jesus or calling around for a job, I go exploring. I go to a bluebonnet festival in a small town called Ennis. These Texas state flowers look like upside-down, pioneer style bonnets. I am having lunch at a place called the Wildflower Café. I meet a woman named Shirley and her daughter who is a pastor, at their invitation I sit down beside them. Sitting nearby is a couple who tells me about their church in Waxahachie. I am sorry when lunch comes to an end, I have been warmed by their welcome. God put them there to make me feel less lonely. I am getting a sense of how God takes care of his children. How he steers us in the right direction, how he places people on the path with us when we need them, and how he is constantly hovering over us.

Summer comes early in Dallas. I visit the Dallas Arboretum in April, and the grounds are already full of tulips bursting with color. I have dinner in the middle of a peach orchard, a long table with strangers for friends. I spend a lot of evenings sitting on my balcony watching the sunset over the baseball field next door.

I go to a concert called "Ella & Louis" at the Meyerson Symphony Center. Byron Stripling, from the Columbus Jazz Orchestra, is conducting and becomes a salve for my homesickness. I go to see Duran Duran at the Music Hall at Fair Park and for a few hours, I sink back into the 80s. I take the train from Addison to Denton for the Arts & Jazz Festival. It has dropped from 80 to 50 degrees and as the winds blow fiercely over the plains, I am swept up in the sounds of Aaron Neville and his band. I am living in one of those endless summers of my childhood.

May comes around and it's time for my annual trip with my travel buddies. My friends and I had been traveling together since 2013. This year we are headed to Cuba. It is the first I would be traveling with them since I have become a Christian and I am slightly anxious. Most of them aren't Christians, and they only know me as the partying prodigal I had been. I wondered if they would still accept me or worse, if they would even notice that I had changed at all. I'm not ashamed for them to know but I don't want to be preachy or judge them in any way. I want to enjoy myself even though I feel on guard most of the time. Should I drink the rum that flows freely with each meal? Should I display my desire to flirt with these gorgeous Cuban men? Would it make me less of a Christian if I do?

The heat is palpable as we pass by colorful buildings, peeling paint revealing the history of this beautiful place. We tour our normal style of haunts; La Cabaña fort, La Necrópolis de Cristóbal Colón, Gran Teatro, and religious sites like Iglesia del Santo Angel Custodio. We go see a show at the famous Tropicana Club and ride around the streets in classic cars.

We explore Finca Vigía, where Ernest Hemingway had lived during his years in Cuba. While there, the tour guide questions my admiration for the man who had written his most famous works there. He had not been kind to women during his lifetime, and he killed animals for wall trophies. With hesitant conviction, I respond that it was his prolific writing skills and his larger-than-life persona that I admire. What I don't tell the guide was that at one point in my life I had also admired his choice to go out on his own terms. That admiration had turned to sympathy as I grew older. He had been a complex human being.

My true test comes when we visit a house where they perform a Santeria ceremony. They pass around food as the practitioner explains the religion and its origins. Then we stand in a circle and start dancing as men beat on batá drums. For the most part, it's all for show, for these curious guests wishing to peek behind the curtain of a religion not prominent in the states. As we dance around, a woman in the crowd starts jerking and flailing her arms around. I start to feel a weight pressing down inside of me and want nothing more then to get out of that house. I walk out and stand near our bus while the others continue to watch in fascination.

When I get home from Cuba, I feel the same emptiness I always do when I return from a trip, a sharp reminder that I have no one to come home to. There is no news about a job opportunity, and I long to be back there with my friends instead of back in reality where my bank account is getting smaller and smaller.

The anxiety floods me, and I cry out for "Egypt" again, I long for the place of my "captivity"—to be back in Cincinnati surrounded by friends who know me well, close to my family . . . to go back to what is familiar. Now I am bored of my stretched-out days, bored with walking around the park and spending the afternoon in the pool. I want to feel productive again. It was then that I get a call from the company I had flown in to interview with, a position had opened up.

I sat in the training sessions staring out at the sun. Now that I am back to work, I want to be back outside, not in here in this typical corporate atmosphere. My new office dulls quickly, and there are only a couple of people I seem to be connecting with. I am used to being in a leader position and it had been since the early days of my career that I had been in a position like this. Not to mention the salary isn't enough to pay all my bills. I am disappointed with the job God has provided for me. Had God brought me here for this? Still, I see it as direction from him. If I am going to have to start all over on the career ladder, find a cheaper apartment, whatever, I am still going to follow him wherever he leads.

I love Covenant church. I go every Sunday, volunteer in the coffee shop, and go to Bible study each Wednesday evening no matter how tired I am from the workday. I miss walking in the sun, I miss the sound of children's laughter at play, I miss the ease of having no place to go. Mostly, I miss the hours I can write. My inspiration has been renewed here and I am back to daily journaling. Meanwhile, God had other plans for me.

My savings had been spent and my income isn't enough to stay where I am. I speak to my sisters on the phone, and I long to be back with them. My soul becomes unsettled once more. I love my new city, and I love my church. I have interviewed at other marketing agencies, but no one is calling me back. It seems God is asking me to take another leap of faith. I quit the new job that took only a few weeks to hate. I pack my car and head back to Ohio.

Some of the happiest days of my adult life are those months in Dallas. I walked with Jesus. I talked to him and felt an immense overwhelming love. He had a protective arm around me, and he wanted nothing more than to spend time with me. Even now, when I should be worried about what tomorrow will bring, I hear him whisper; "I got you . . . I love you . . . and I won't let you down . . . ever." The thing that has changed since I have been in Dallas is that now I believe him.

I knew I would miss Dallas, but Dallas would remain in my heart. I'd look back on that time in my life as a time of lying in green pastures; the empty days listening to the children playing in the sun, walking with Jesus, and knowing tomorrow I would do the same. That freedom . . . that feeling of healing. I had been emptied and was ready to fill up again. I knew then as I walked those miles that I would never have that back, that I would miss these days once they were gone. And I was right, there are times I ache for them. They were the only thing I had, and they were enough. Walking with Jesus, his arm wrapped around me as I cried my fears out to him.

Before I leave Dallas, I purge most of the stuff that had been moving around with me all these years. I throw away paperwork from previous jobs, old love letters, and pictures of men who are no longer in my life. I keep only my words, important photos and the clothes and shoes I wear on a regular basis. It was long overdue; I had been holding on to too many physical relics of my life.

I take most of my books to Half Price Books and add buffer to my bank account. The multiple boxes had added too much weight to move around all these years. I keep a few books that were too important to let go of. The rest could now have their spines cracked, their pages bent, their ink sniffed, instead of sitting in unopened boxes for years.

I take my unused handbags, some barely worn shoes, and old clothes to the Goodwill down the street. The tarot cards and Ouija board are left abandoned on my empty bedroom floor. It not just physical items I leave behind, the bitterness in my heart stays behind in that park silenced beneath the sound of children's laughter.

At first I didn't understand why God sent me to Dallas but it would become an essential part of my return. While there, Jesus took my heart and reshaped it, tearing down walls, healing scars, and repairing the damage that had taken place over the past twenty years. I had to be far away from where I had been for this to happen. My soul had found its way back home, now the rest of me would follow.

Return: come or go back to a place or person.

Restoration: the action of returning something to a former owner, place, or condition.

Renewal: the replacing or repair of something that is worn out, run-down, or broken.

Reawakening: emerge or cause to emerge again

7

Whispers in the Wilderness

On the other hand, I am writing a new commandment to you, which is true in Him and in you, because the darkness is passing away and the true Light is already shining.

—*1 John 2:8 NASB*

No one is rooting for you more than I am.

—*God*

IT'S A FIFTEEN-HOUR DRIVE between Dallas and Columbus, Ohio. I am making the drive back less than six months after the fifteen-hour drive that got me there. I am driving back lighter, I feel renewed, restored, and relieved of past burdens I had been holding on to. Back in Columbus, I wait five months for another job. I don't know why God is making me wait as if he is holding out on me. I say, "I trust you, Lord" but I am full of anxiety. I try to encourage myself; he will make a way for me . . . he will provide the answers I need. "Let not your heart be troubled" (*but it is!*) Still, I won't turn away from him. I won't give up. I won't run away just because it's difficult. He had promised that he would provide, he has promised restoration for the career I have stepped away from. I am still adrift on the ocean but this time the waters around me are still.

Change and uncertainty are scary, this holds true for even the most seasoned of Christians. A lot of people choose not to move away from their current situations because of not knowing what awaits on the other side. Giving up control of your life and letting God lead may feel like you are jumping off a cliff. I spent many days wondering where I would live and when I would get a new job. The one thing I never had to wonder about was where I was going to attend church. They just seemed to come to me, as if someone leads me straight through their doors.

When I first move back, I start attending a church called Victorious Living. It's smaller than the church in Dallas. I quickly get to know the people there on a personal level. I might have to wait on a solution to make a living, but I don't have to wait for a church that quickly feels like home. I still don't know the words to these contemporary Christian songs, but I always felt the spirit during the worship part of the service. There are communion tables in both corners up front and I love having the opportunity to partake in the old, familiar ritual. It is evident something inside me has changed from my teenage-filled hesitation.

The parade floats are lined up along Southwest Blvd. The early September weather is warm with a sun-lit glow. She stands there with a group of young girls surrounding her; she somehow looks the same even though at least ten years have gone by since we have spoken to one another. I had been the maid of honor at her wedding all those years ago. She watches me walk across the street to her. I am anxious as the anger, guilt, and regret comes back to me. I can't seem to recall our last conversation; we had drifted away from one another. She glances down at my t-shirt which had the VLC logo on it. She is as surprised by that as of the fact that I am standing in front of her. She tells me she is there with her own church where she is a youth group leader. I am both shocked and uplifted at the thought that both of us are now active members of a church. Somewhere within the years that separated us we have found our way to Jesus. We greet each other with open arms right there beside the crepe-papered, banner-toting, hay wagons. I sense the sweet forgiveness of our fractured friendship.

I am attending a weekend conference at my church. A guest pastor from City of Grace has come to preach. He tells the congregation that we have been sent here on purpose for a purpose and I feel a churning begin inside me. After he is done preaching, he asks if anyone wants to come up to be prophesied over, most of us walk up and we form a line. Even though I have sought out psychics and mediums my entire life, I am inexplicably uncertain about this. He goes down the line praying over people. As he gets closer to me, I feel my stomach start to tremble and my heart begins to race. He places both hands on top of my head and speaks in a tongue I don't understand. He opens his eyes and tells me: "I see eyes that are illuminated. Like Superman, how rays would come out of his eyes, I saw illumination coming out of your eyes, through prophetic dreams and visions. You can see into the realm of the spirit. What they used to call prophets in the Old Testament, today we call them seers. God showed me you have this ability to see." I say nothing, I just stand there and tremble. Although not completely surprised by what he has told me, I wonder how I will use this ability for the glory of God.

"You already know what God wants you to do." A prayer partner tells me. I have a sneaky suspicion that my purpose has to do with writing. Perhaps I will write song lyrics that would be sung in church, put together Bible studies, urge readers to pursue a life in Christ through poetic prose, or share my prodigal testimony. I don't yet have clarity in the direction God is leading. The senior pastor tells me; "there is still a weight you are carrying but soon you will be like a hot-air balloon, and you will lift off." One thing is becoming clear, God is starting to point me toward my purpose.

I had come back when the summer sun was still high in the sky. The leaves are changing now, and an ex-boyfriend knocks on the door. We had "dated" when we were thirteen, and by "dated" I mean we walked around the neighborhood holding hands. Back then, I had developed a crush on another boy, and we drifted apart. By the time he was twenty, he had met someone else and married her. We saw each other again once in our early twenties but I hadn't heard from him since. He looks the same but older. Old desire flares up and I'm tempted…really tempted. We don't sleep together but I am disappointed with how easily I could sway back into sin. I don't know if I would've said no if he would have asked and that troubles me. How easily I could betray the friend I had spent months in Dallas getting to know. Perhaps, we hadn't become as close as I thought we had. This is my first temptation after my return. I guiltily ask God for forgiveness and soldier on, continuing to read my Bible, and being active in church. I ignore the hissing in my ear; "You will never change." I had though. I attend a church on the weekends instead of going to a bar. I speak differently. My biggest fear isn't that I will change, it's that I won't. I'm trying to get hooked on so tight so that I won't float away this time.

In the fall of 2018, I start attending a different church. As much as I was hoping I had become immune to love, I begin to develop feelings for someone and quickly fall into an old pattern. Crossroads Church holds their services in a small movie theatre inside a mall, I'm beginning to know the words to these new songs. The pastor is young and single. During a prayer night, after I have finished praying, I look up to see him sitting cross-legged on the stage. He has his Bible opened on his lap with his head bowed over it. I hear a voice that sounds like mine say something that surprises me; "God, if you want to send me a husband, let him love you as much as this man does." What??!! That didn't come from me! I have sworn off men, love has done enough damage to me! I can't deny it though as something starts to stir inside me after that prayer night. I convinced myself that God was putting these feelings inside me for a reason.

I have been praying for my purpose and hoping God will direct me to write a book or travel around sharing my prodigal testimony. Instead, I begin to dream about becoming a pastor's wife. God is digging up something inside of me that I don't want to unbury. I don't want to fall in love again. I hear his voice; "I need you to believe in something that you swore you'd never believe in again. To have faith in the one thing that has disappointed you time and time again. I am asking you to trust in me, that I will be there for you no matter what happens." I am so confused and disappointed about this change in direction that I don't speak to God for twenty-four hours.

My prayers turn into words I never thought I would ever say, I'm praying for God to turn me into a Proverbs 31 type of woman. I will put aside my own talents and dreams of writing and stand in the shadows behind a pastor if God asks me to do so. Besides, this was how I was raised it's supposed to be between a man and a woman. Even before I get to know the pastor better, I make him into an illusion. He's humble, funny, and has kind eyes. He also writes beautifully which endears him to me more. When we hug for the first time, I get all shaky. I have forgotten how nice it is to have "butterflies" in my stomach. The more I get to know him though, the more my feelings hesitate. Relationships have always been better in my imagination than they are in real-life. I ignore my intuition, though. I firmly believe that God wants me to fall in love with this man, even though I harbor mixed feelings. I pray with sweat and tears for seven months. I am as humble before God as I have ever been. As weeks go on and nothing happens, I start to panic. Perhaps, I think, I don't recognize God's voice after all.

When I discover that the pastor has started seeing someone, I cry knowing my heart will become fractured again. I had followed God to Dallas and then back home. I had given up my career, how could love (God) do this to me yet again?? I wasn't crushed because I didn't get the guy. I'm crushed because I feel like God had set me up. I'm more disappointed in the thought that God would do this to me than the thought of not getting the life I was imagining. Would God ask me to open my heart only to leave it empty? Satan is watching from the sidelines, certain that this is going to take me down.

After all this time, all those months in Dallas, is it possible that I still don't recognize the voice of God? My desires turn from the imaginary relationship to my very real relationship with God. I start reading books by other Christians to help me work through identifying God's voice. I'm hungry to hear it, no matter what it says. I am desperate for God not desperate for a man.

I had let my heart out of its cage and the fact that I could open it to the possibility of love again was progress. God had used a common pattern from my past to show me that I need to surrender *all* my heart to *him*. He will hold it together no matter what or who tries to break it.

I am on an afternoon walk around the neighborhood. The sun is high, its warmth and comfort sinks into my skin. I am listening to a Christian playlist when I sense another heartbeat inside my own. Something much like the light summer breeze flows through me from head to toe. A rush of joy overtakes me, and I twirl like a young girl in the middle of this neighborhood street; arms and heart spread wide open.

8

The Blood on my Hands

I have swept away your offenses like a cloud,
your sins like the morning mist.
Return to me, for I have redeemed you.

—*Isa 44:22 NIV*

Did my prodigal years change the purpose for my life?

THE QUESTION HANGS THERE in the center of my mind. The big *what if* of my life. What if I had not walked away? I don't know how God would have used me if I would have stayed and I can't go back and find out. It's pointless to stand here asking, though. All I can do is plea with him to use me now. All I can do is give the rest of my years over to him.

Will I have to eventually pay for all the things I had done?

It's dusty, it's dry, and they had been walking for years. They had a simple request for water. Moses strikes a rock instead of speaking

34

to it and because of that one decision he won't be entering the promised land with the Israelites. Ouch—sounds kind of harsh. David hands the building plans for the temple over to his son. The shadows of their past sins linger over their lives. Will it be the same for me?

Do I have blood on my hands?

What of those souls who I helped the snake lure away when I was out there serving him? Did I deter people away from God? Is their blood staining my hands? Did that atheist couple I met ever come to believe? Would I get an opportunity to introduce someone to Jesus, or did I miss my chance?

Is God not answering my prayer for a kingdom purpose because he doesn't trust me with it?

I mean, why would he? I had written many songs in his name when I was a teenager fresh up from the altar. And what had I done with them? I put them in a trunk to fade away with the years. God had given me a desire to write, and I have wasted it. I want to do something *big* for God. I know that being a witness and living a godly life is every Christian's purpose, but I want to *leave a mark*. An even deeper question rises to the surface; *would God ever dangle a carrot stick in front of me only to yank it up?*

Am I as valuable as those Christians who have served God all their lives?

I am envious as I watch Christians who have followed God all their lives. They are living out their purpose with flourish. They seem to get opportunity after opportunity to demonstrate their faith. I might have missed my chance. As if, since I wasted so many years, nothing would come of my life. I will not get to participate in work for the kingdom. Am I too late? I had spent too many years working for the snake, I didn't have a lifetime in front of me to work for

God. Knowing this, I couldn't help but ask *will my dream be left unfulfilled?*

> For I know the plans I have for you, declares the LORD, plans to prosper you and not to harm you, plans to give you hope and a future.
>
> —*Jeremiah 29:11 NIV*

Do I have a score to settle with God?

The sun goes dark as a man gasps his last intake of air. He is nailed to an old cross on a hill that resembles a skull. He is there so I don't have to be. Three days go by when this same man sees the light shine into a dark tomb, the stone barring the entrance is no longer there. He steps out into the sun, breathing as he was before. He is not the gardener.

Imagining that scene makes me want to carry around all the guilt and shame I deserve. I want to regret the life I lived. But there is no shame when I look back. I can't erase my past, but I can move forward in God's grace and go where he leads me.

I want to persuade someone not to turn their back on God. If they have already walked away, I want to persuade them to come back. It's not enough for me to just be back with him, I want to make a kingdom mark on the world before I go. I still have time to leave my God-given legacy.

Staring out a window and watching snow slide off the rooftop next door, I know I am not where I am meant to be. I am wasting my time and my life. There are a few other Christians here in the office building where I work, but we are secluded in individual offices. I barely see anyone during the day except for the cleaning lady. We talk about our mutual friend, Jesus. We share how our Sunday services went, and gospel songs we like. Our conversations are a respite in this dull atmosphere that leaves me feeling like a zombie at the end of each day. If my dream of doing something specific for the kingdom doesn't come to fruition, will I end up more bitter than I was before? I had let God down, surely, he will do the same to me.

I watch Priscilla Shirer, Lisa Harper, Jennie Allen, and all those other women who travel, write books, and speak at various events. I want to do the same. I want to spread the gospel like they are doing and share my testimony with the world. I wish someone would look at me and say, "I want what she has". I want people to see my unabashed love for Jesus—like those faithful women who have already succeeded in a place I want to succeed.

I don't want to walk into heaven with the smell of smoke on my clothes, any remnants clinging on from my prodigal years. But I am afraid to ask God for anything. I didn't use my resources for him before, is that the reason he is not blessing me with opportunities now? I had denied his existence. I doubt his goodness since I am so undeserving of it. Yet, I remind myself, he built his church upon someone who had denied him.

I often think of Peter. I want to know what it's like to walk on water. I want to know what the voice of Jesus sounded like. But I have more pertinent questions for him; *What was it like to carry your guilt around? Better yet, how did it feel when you understood that He didn't hold it against you?*

God takes the bad and uses it for our good and his glory. Perhaps my life has not been in vain, perhaps telling my own story will bring a sheep back into the fold or keep someone from walking away.

If you met me years ago and I told you God doesn't exist, that he doesn't matter, or that Jesus was just another human being . . . I take it back. I would say something different now. I can't rewind time back to our conversation so let me say it here: *I was wrong.*

The snake starts to hiss . . .
What are you doing?
You can't do this.
You don't deserve this.
Do you think anything will turn out differently for you?
I start to question . . .
Who could I have been?
Do I still have time to do enough for God?
Can I make it up to him?
Have I wasted my life?
God reassures . . .
There's more coming.
There is something for you to do.
Don't give up the dream I have placed inside of you.
Don't stop believing in me now.

9

The Beauty in the Ashes

Are your wonders known in the place of darkness,
or your righteous deeds in the land of oblivion?

—*Ps 88:12 NIV*

IT'S A SUNDAY MORNING in 1997 and out of boredom, curiosity, or both, I find myself walking through the doors of a church called Mountview Christian. It's a beautiful building from the outside, and I discover its interior is just as inviting. My childhood years come flooding back. The hard wooden pews have been cushioned, a baptistry is located to the left of the stage, and there are offering envelopes placed strategically in the seats. The light falling on the pews through the stained-glass windows brings a warm sensation to my soul. People approach me and take my hand in theirs. We sing songs from purple hymn books with the church name embossed on the cover. I still know all the words. No matter how hard I try to run or hide from my childhood upbringing, it is still there within me. God has not left me, even though I have left him.

In January 2007 my family is shattered by an unexpected tragedy. In August of the same year, my live-in boyfriend tells me he doesn't want to be with me anymore. A few months later my father dies of cancer. Life as I know it goes up in smoke yet again. I seek solace in God, because quite frankly, I know nothing else will help. I filled my ears with the Christian artists from my teenage years, and the southern gospel bands my parents were so fond of. If I only had the courage to turn back to him. Still, I wanted to do life on my own terms, and I refused to surrender. I longed for the comfort that God offered, but I was unwilling to change what he would've wanted to change in my life.

As research for this book, I read through my journals from the 90s and early 2000s. I know what I will find there. Their faces are still fresh in my mind. I recall the angry words, the alcohol-induced fights, but there were also scenes of love that had made a valiant effort. In the journals, I find the part of me before disappointment turned into bitterness. Nothing I find on the pages is unexpected except for the perpetual conversation I have been having with God. Throughout my entire adult life, I have run to him in anguish, I have shaken my fists at the sky. There were times I cried out for God to save me, other times I didn't want him there. I didn't want him to see what I had done so I stayed hidden in the shadows. I cried out to him when I was drunk, and the next day when I was hungover. I cried out to him when I met someone I desperately wanted to be with, then again when I wanted that same someone gone. I would randomly listen to the Christian songs of my youth whenever I felt I was drowning. Without fail they would lift my spirit; I knew hope was there waiting for me to latch on to it. I knew God was hovering even when I claimed he didn't exist at all.

A few wolves in sheep's clothing came knocking at my door during those prodigal years. One of my past lovers wouldn't shut up about God. He called himself a Christian even though he was living with me. A co-worker spoke to me about God one evening, and then invited me to his house since his wife was away. When I realized I didn't have to be afraid of God the same way I fear walking down an alley by myself, I was flooded with relief. God would never be inappropriate toward me, never degrade me, nor lie to me. I am safe here. It took some time to forgive those men from my past. I eventually did, every single one of them. When I looked back to reread my journals, they no longer had a grasp on me.

When I looked back at my prodigal years I was able to look back without shame. I see with remarkable clarity that there has indeed been a change in me. The change didn't happen overnight though, it took a trip through Dallas and a few lessons of faith. God had to take me away from everything and everyone I knew and do some major work in my heart. I didn't know how important those few months would be in my life, but I would look back on them time and time again. Those early days of my return would always be a reminder of God's constant love, protection, and provision.

Going through my old journals didn't bring on the nostalgia I feared, the shame I expected, nor bring an uncertainty about my decision to return. It wasn't all dark back there; I enjoyed living a single, childless life. I had been the life of the party, I traveled extensively, and I built a successful career. But looking back through all those pages, I realized how grateful I am to be back home.

Oh, the grace of God
The exquisite beauty of Him
For the thought of angelic beings taking us to heaven
Straight from life to Jesus
Straight from pain, weariness
to a tree with unyielding fruit
To a crystal sea
And a river of life
Oh, why does our soul not leap from our skin
And soar there now?
How we hold our breath for the last one
For the next life to come—our eternal home!
Oh, for the grace of God go I
Straight from life . . . to LIFE.

10

In the Valley of the Shadow of Death

...the people living in darkness
have seen a great light;
on those living in the land of the shadow of death
a light has dawned.

—*Matt 4:16 NIV*

THE STING OF DEATH is constantly searing my skin. It happens
every time I take a whiff inside a cedar wood box. I am back there
in the gift shop at Carter Caves in Kentucky. She is there . . . always she is there. I lost my mom on a sunny April morning in
1999. She has been gone over twenty years. In a couple of years,
I will have lived just as long without her as I did with her here.
She had suffered for years from heart disease and diabetes. I have
the unwanted memory of heating up bags for her to do kidney
dialysis. I conjure up that last scene; her face as white as paper
and me turning from her lifeless body as an uncle takes me in his
arms. That was the day the sun dimmed. This is the cut in my life.
The wound that would never heal. Even now sometimes I cross
through a random room and the thought of her overtakes me, my

breath catches as a lump begins to form in my throat. In a hospital room in the middle of the city, a stranger picks up a Gideon Bible, reads the name Opal Fairchild and wonders; *who was this woman with the name of a gemstone?* That is how my mother lives on, her name etched on Bibles dedicated to the hospital where we left her . . . where she left us. She is forever etched on my heart.

I am a coal miner's daughter. I didn't know him when he worked beneath the ground, during his younger years living in Butcher Hollow, Kentucky. I knew him later as someone who would come home every night with the smell of blacktop on his work boots, browned from the sun. Eight years after my mother crossed the veil my father joined her. His many years of smoking caught up to him. I didn't visit him during his final days. The last time we saw each other his smile was so full of love. I didn't want that image erased by him whittling away. I think of him whenever I see a box of Little Debbie Oatmeal Cream Pies. Sometimes I catch a whiff of cherry tobacco as if he is nearby still smoking his pipe.

Does time heal all wounds? I don't know, it still feels sharp when I think of them both. My sisters and I carried on. They had kids to raise. I had my career. A decade would go by before death came for us again.

A redheaded boy is doing BMX tricks in the Kmart parking lot, spinning the bike beneath him as if gravity isn't a factor. His name is Brian, but we call him Howdy. Him and I were fifteen when we started hanging around each other and he started coming over to the house. He was from a broken home and our home was always full of love. Him and my sister married in 1992. In 2010 he was diagnosed with a rare form of sarcoma. We were told he wouldn't be with us much longer. He had surgeries, chemo, and traveled around to various specialists. He started looking decades older than he was, his hair grew back in grey. He no longer looked like Howdy Doody. Every holiday we were told it would be his last. He was prayed for, and anointed by church elders as we waited for heaven to step in. He refused to give up and never wavered in his faith for the seven years he suffered. He crossed over the veil the weekend before I moved to Dallas. I fly back for his memorial service and see my sister sitting at a table by herself. She looks utterly lost. She doesn't seem to notice what is going on around her. She offers me a small smile, this baby sister she has barely seen over the past few years.

When I come back to Ohio, I move in with her. She attends a few grief sessions which doesn't seem to help. Her friends and church community try to counsel her, but all she sees is a future he won't be in. "If God loves me, why would he let this happen to me?" Numb from her grief she refuses to move on even as the rest of the world moves on around her. She doesn't want to make new memories; she wants to relive the old ones.

As the gusty wind blows outside my small office window, I think of her. She is home alone, missing her husband in excruciating pain. I wonder; does she wish she were dead also, her body turned to ashes mixed in with his? The thought causes a tightness in my chest, a heavy heart weighing down the rest of me. We have had different experiences with love. Her relationship ended with a comma, all of mine ended with periods. How does one continue the relationship when the other has crossed over? She is caught in a moment she cannot move on from. She sits deep in her grief; it wraps her like a warm hug from him. My nephew resembles his father so much, it's hard to believe it's not my old friend standing there in the hallway.

I wake up in a boutique hotel called The Pack and Carriage, in my favorite city in the world. The cherry on top of my birthday vacation, or "holiday" as they say over here, will be spending the day at Highclere Castle. My phone buzzes with a text. It's my oldest sister asking if I can call her. I have Verizon travel pass, so I call, it's one a.m. in the states and something must be wrong. "Ted had a heart attack last night. He didn't make it." Ted. Her husband, Ted. My other brother-in-law. I can only respond by saying "Your Ted?" The shock of it is inexplicable. We are only two years from my other brother-in-law's death. I had two, now I have none. My flight home is the next day, so I continue with my excursion to the castle but now there is a heavy weight upon my chest. I am awed by the splendor of the castle, all the scenes from Downton Abbey floating around in my mind. Back on the bus though, I stare out the window completely dismayed by my sister's news. I don't want to go back and face yet another death. At Ted's funeral I watch as my sister quivers uncontrollably, a son on each side, they take her hands in theirs. Their family has shrunk. She seems more vulnerable than she used to. Her face looks overcast, and she always seems to hesitate before she smiles.

I mention my sisters first when I pray, I can't imagine their grief. They must adjust to life without their husbands; car repairs, appliance breakdowns, parenting young adults . . . they now must face it alone. God had sent me back to Ohio to be here during this time, but there isn't anything I can do. There is nothing I can offer to comfort them. I cannot bring their husbands, their lives, their planned futures back to them. My four nephews are left behind without fathers, the last one will graduate without his father looking on. I can't ease the pain. I can't even make a dent in it. My family is overwhelmed with grief, and we can't help but wonder, *where is God amid our pain?*

It's June 2021 and my oldest sister has taken her sons to Florida. I am watching her house and taking care of her dogs. I look over at the couch where Ted was when he died. I stumble up against the wall and break down in tears, crying so hard I am gasping for breath. I sense a presence there, I hear that voice which has become so familiar to me; "You are grieving too, my child."

To my cousin, Gene:

An old red barn sits in the middle of a snow dusted field, a common sight in the Midwest. To me, it is a reminder of a cold night in January 2007. The thought of you in your final moments in a cold barn unsettles us, and we wonder if you were alone. Only God knows what happened there. Neither way would be easy for us. I think perhaps if we knew you didn't decide this for yourself that it would make us feel only slightly better. That you weren't so unhappy with life that you ended it. There were visible rope burns on your neck, laying there in the casket as all of us walked by.

It had been about five years since I had spoken to you. The last time being our parents' wedding; my aunt, your uncle. It turned us into more than cousins, we were stepsiblings now. That was the only time in my entire life when I got to hang out with just you. We went to our grandma's house even though she hasn't been alive for sixteen years. The same house where we played Red Rover and put on Christmas plays in the barn. I am glad that she, nor my mother were here to see those rope burns. I remember our younger selves performing gymnastics on a mattress in the middle of the floor. I see your fingers behind my head in a photo making "rabbit ears". I remember your goofy way, relentless pestering, and your laugh.

I was afraid to look in my backseat for months after you left us. I was afraid I would see you sitting back there, your neck at a weird angle. You have stayed with us, even though you have been gone for so long. We take you with us to the annual family reunion at Carter Caves, where you once walked with us down the path to the cold cave to escape the sweltering August heat. Red Rover, Red Rover. Way too soon, you went over.

There have been aunts, uncles, friends, etc. who have passed away, but these are the deaths I carry around with me. Every death that happens now, we feel tenfold. I try to think of Mary and Martha, how they cried for their brother and how Jesus cried with them. What we are promised of who God is near to. It is a difficult thing to watch grief day in and day out. My sisters feel cheated out of futures which had felt so secure. They hurt for their children who must live the rest of their lives without their fathers. Sorrow is a deep, deep well and we are drowning in it.

We can't even begin to imagine or think on the same level with God. Where we see life, he sees a temporary state for us. Where we see death, he sees a transition to a higher plane. It's hard to imagine how many souls will be in heaven, we can't comprehend the capacity. Those who have been here already and those who exist here now. Those who have evaporated into thin air or climbed in to chariots and rode away on the wind. We return to "dust" but only our flesh. Sometimes watching church online with my sister, I sense a wind sweeping through the room . . . Jesus is here. God stays close to the broken hearted. Though he is always with us, the grief filled broken heart experiences a different level of his love, proof of his promise that *in this shadowed valley a light has dawned.*

Unveil the heavens and darken the stars
Oh, come Lord
Shake the heavens and move the seas
Oh, come Lord
Roll back the sky like a scroll
Oh, come Lord
send down the new Jerusalem
raise the bodies long in the graves
bring forth the ashes of loved ones
fill the earth with your glory
and make all things new
Oh, come Lord
that we may see you.

11

Of Jasper Walls and a Glass Sea

Then I saw a new heaven and a new earth,
for the first heaven and the first earth had passed away...

—Rev 21:1 NIV

I AM SITTING OUTSIDE a café eating lobster on my 46th birthday. Before me stands the Palais Garnier, its architecture is beyond stunning; shiny, ornate, golden. Everything I expected of Paris has proven true, it is indeed a magical city. There are many places to explore here, and I only have a few days. I take a train out to the Palace of Versailles and gawk at its grandeur, I gaze up at the Eiffel Tower, and cross over bridges that boast the finest sculptures. A few days before on this mini tour of Europe, I had stood looking out over the shimmering waters of Lake Geneva. Between the two scenes I ponder heaven: more elaborate than Versailles' grand hallways, more majestic than the water that falls from the Swiss Alps. It is hard to imagine, but I believe. And I want to see it someday.

God instilled in me a wandering spirit and curious mind which has taken me from the Emerald Isle to the Negev desert. I have stood beside the Sea of Galilee picturing Jesus taking a walk, dipped my hand in the River of Jordan, and have been inside an empty tomb. I have strolled through beautiful historic buildings like Rosslyn Chapel, Canterbury Cathedral, and Notre Dame. I have stood in the snow dusted Carpathian Mountains, climbed on Mayan ruins, and have listened to bagpipes in the Scotland Highlands. I have discovered that America is indeed beautiful, from the glaciers of Alaska to the lighthouses in Maine and everywhere in between. I love this incredible earth but sometimes I get so desperate for heaven.

I long to be able to peek across the veil like John the Revelator. Mansions, streets of gold, and crystal-like seas await. Heaven, in my imagination, has a lush garden I can walk around in while carrying on a conversation with a sleek, black jaguar. I don't know if there will be jaguars there, but if there are I hope they can talk. In this vision of mine, a waterfall flows from the heavens down to the new earth. People I haven't hugged for decades will be there. The ancient saints I have read about are walking around. They turn toward me and say, "Oh, it's you. We were cheering you on."

I want to hear how the angels sound when they sing. Look upon the entire creation as we worship the way we should. I want to hear the music that is in God's ears. When I get caught up in listening to worship music, it takes me to a different place. I get a small taste of what heaven might be like.

The stories I read in the Bible turn into biographies of my Christian brothers and sisters who walked this earth before me. It is a history book, a poetry book, guidance for my everyday life, and ultimately, the greatest love story of all time. There are many stories in the Bible that take my breath away but imagining the story of those three young Hebrew men walking around in a fire (with that unidentified fourth man, wink wink), and then walking out *without even the smell of smoke on their clothes.* Whew! I feel that story from my head to my toes!

My prayers reach heaven, even the ones that may seem too small to bother God with. Deep winter in Ohio and exposed pipes under the house presents no rivalry. The water in our house had been frozen for several days. I was on a winter hike in a metro park (*I don't know why either*) when I prayed over a frozen puddle asking God to unfreeze our water. A few minutes later my sister calls to say the water in our house had thawed. I have prayed over a dishwasher and a furnace when there was no money to replace them. I go to God with bigger petitions. He has provided opportunities for me to serve in a local non-profit organization and has allowed me to lead an online Bible study. He has given me time and a direction to write this book. I asked, he answered. I sought, I found. I knocked and he has opened doors for me.

It's Spring 2020 and the world has turned on its head. On top of family grief, a virus, and violence it is hard to feel hopeful about anything. The weight of it all has me in tears. Tomorrow is Easter and the doors to the church are closed. During the night, though, something has resurrected inside me. I wake with images of an empty tomb and a stone out of place. Death has been conquered and all this world's suffering is temporary. I feel such a sweet and ecstatic joy come over me. What would social media look like this morning if it had been around? It is the biggest news story in our history. Not only did Jesus arise, but he also saved us from *our own death*. All this time I sought after supernatural events, spirits that lived beyond the veil, and it was *right there*. Taught to me from my earliest of days. Rising from the dead! Miracle healings! People who defied the odds! People who never died! Unlike pandemics of the past, we have the internet to stay connected during this one. I tuned into Elevation Church, and they debut a song called "Rattle", the lyrics are about dry bones coming back to life. I could have shouted from the rooftops!

Sometimes I just stare up at the sky. I know that one day the heavens will roll back like a scroll. I picture Jesus up there, arms outstretched. The image makes me want to jump out of my skin!

We are just one heartbeat away from God. Although you are always in his presence, and he is always with you, in *that moment* of your so-called death you will be with him in a new way you can't even imagine. You are safely in the arms of Jesus, no matter what is happening. I'm not saying you won't experience bad things in life, you will . . . that's life. I will suffer loss (again), potentially another broken relationship, but it's different now. I have met the Prince of Peace, and no matters what happens I have direct access to that kind of peace . . . you know, the one that passes all understanding. I have figured out why my mother used to shout in that church pew. Sometimes, heaven comes down.

12

Salt and Light

You are the salt of the earth . . . You are the light of the world. A town built on a hill cannot be hidden. Neither do people light a lamp and put it under a bowl. Instead, they put it on its stand, and it gives light to everyone in the house.

—Matt 5:13-16 NIV

SHE STANDS THERE IN the rain without an umbrella, without a voice. People pass by her as if she isn't even there. Her face is lined, her clothes are dirty, her hair is matted. She looks both ways before she crosses the street to McDonalds in hopes a kind stranger will throw some change her way. I pull up close to her and our eyes meet. I hand her an umbrella and a five-dollar bill, and I wonder where she will go when I leave her.

One morning as I am in the drive thru for breakfast, a gentleman approaches my car. It's always me, never the man in front of me. I am less intimidating. This makes me so angry that when he asks me for money, I blatantly ignore him. He asks again, louder but still politely. I make a motion with my hands as if to brush him aside, as if to *dismiss him*. His need is not as important as me getting my breakfast. *He is not as important as me.* He walks over to another car, leaving me with guilt and conviction in my heart. I make up excuses in my head; I'm allowed to be in a bad mood especially before I have had breakfast. I tithe regularly, I donate clothes and money to charities. I can't be generous to everyone who asks.

A man is hanging out by the market where I go to get my lunch. As I come out, he tells me he is thirsty and asks if I can help him out. My first response is a quick no, because quite frankly, I don't carry cash anymore. And if I did, would I dig out some for him anyway? He must not have heard me because he asks me again. The look in his eyes is one of desperation and sadness. I feel as if I must explain (which makes me slightly angry at him for putting me in this position). I tell him I don't have cash. As I drive away it weighs heavy on me. I could have walked back into the store and bought him a drink. I know the living water and I didn't take the opportunity to share it with him.

I have always been conflicted about how to treat homeless people. My thoughts were "they must have done something to put themselves there, they were irresponsible", "If I give them money, they will spend it on drugs." One day, Jesus told me what to do. I start taking cash out each time I get paid and keep some on hand just in case anyone asks me for it. The truth is, it isn't my money, it's God's. If God tells me to give it to someone with a cheerful heart, then that is what I will do. God didn't just open my heart; he has opened my hand.

Back in my prodigal days, my oldest sister brought me a dusty rose Bible with my name on it. She never tired in her efforts to get me back on the right path. I threw it in the dumpster at my apartment complex. An act of defiance I took great pleasure in at the time. Here I am years later, and I can't get enough of it. I even lead a small group online. I read through the Bible in 2017 and recorded all my thoughts, regardless of what they were. God was not surprised by what I had to say. I had *a lot* of questions, some which have been with me since my Sunday school days. Then I started breaking it down, studying the Bible along with books and studies from Lifeway and Proverbs 31. Through this I became engrossed in the stories. I started seeing the people in the stories as the same as me. Their relationship with God was sometimes complicated, one minute they were crying out for him to save them, the next they were dancing in the street. I admired most of them; those boys walking in the fire; the courageous queen; the ones who simply said; "Here I am, send me".

I hated David; you know, the man after God's own heart? I liked the poetic writings in Psalms as much as anyone, though it made him seem wishy-washy to me. I didn't care much for the *you-wasn't-where-you-were-supposed-to-be-so-you-took-a-woman-got-her-pregnate-then-set-her-husband-up-to-be-killed* side of him. I hate that we didn't get to hear Bathsheba's side of the story. The audacity of that man! I know, kettle, pot, and all that, but this was "a man after God's own heart". I avoided the story until one day it was part of a Bible study and I realized what had happened *afterwards*. I read the consequence of his decision. His baby died and he suffered. I saw his humanity and had empathy for him. How disappointed in himself he must've been. He asked forgiveness and he got it from God. It also wasn't lost on me that I am at times wishy-washy with my faith, and that I can't be trusted near temptation either.

As I got into the Bible studies, I became more and more enchanted with these people. Not only did I admire Queen Esther, but also Queen Vashti. I read about female pioneers and leaders throughout the Bible that I once had deemed as underrated. They were never underrated in God's eyes. Them and their stories are just as important as the others. I read all those stories that I did when I was a kid in that basement, but this time they sink in. Instead of people that are far off, they have become people who take walks with me, people who cheer me on—my personal cloud of witnesses. I want to be a part of this kingdom history. I don't wish to be tortured, end up in a prison, or shipwrecked, but I want to be brave and bold if I ever am. I am willing—here I am, send me.

I want to be remembered for serving God. I want the name of Jesus to bring tears to my eyes like Pastor Stephen Hayes, to appear unshakable like Pastor Steven Furtick, to be as determined to tell people about Christ as John Allen Chau. To feel these words within the depths of me; *to live is Christ, but to die is gain.*

The first time I see a good friend after I returned to God, she tells me; "you look so much lighter." There has been a change in me. My chains have been loosened like they were for Paul and Silas. Those prodigal years had turned my life into a heavy weight, one I carried around for way too long.

The crash can be so daunting
can feel like my insides
are ripping in two
and most distressing—
can make me feel
so far from you.
Then a calm sweeps in
to that lowest place
When my cries are heard
by only you.
As I scream, cry out in anguish,
when I am deep in that darkest moment.
Because you come.
Because I feel your spirit
You—my Jehovah Shalom,
Bring a sweet rushing of peace
And I feel released.
This heavenly hug washes over my spirit
Caresses my soul
Wraps invisible hands
Around my heart to hold
it steady
To stop its shaking
To hold me still.
The darkness gives way to light
To renewed hope
To a deeper-rooted strength
Until I become like a tree
Planted by the waters—
my faith grows.

13

In the Gloaming

*The light shines in the darkness, and the darkness
has not overcome it.*

—*John 1:5 NIV*

A subtle hiss from the snake turns into a conversation . . .

*"Don't you miss it? You had fun out there.
Come on, you didn't do anything that bad.
Don't you want to come back to the darkness and play?"*

I had given satan an opening.

Temptation

Sometimes sin doesn't lurk in the shadows.

The same month I was celebrating my one-year return to God, an
old flame walked back into my life. When I say old flame, I mean
the first flame. The first kiss. The first sweaty hand I held walking
around the neighborhood. We were thirteen. We connected once

in our early twenties and then didn't see each other for the next twenty years. He had recently moved away but was back in town for a couple of days. It was nice to see him again, I hadn't kept in touch with many people from my distant past. He had known my parents and had remained friends with my sister all this time. I found his arms to be a familiar place. A long-buried flicker rose to the surface. I wanted the connection. I thought maybe God had brought him back so we could rekindle a flame, but he was married so obviously that wasn't true.

I am a creature of habit and as such have eaten the same breakfast for *years*. I'm not a morning person and therefore breakfast gets picked up on the way to work. You know those McDonalds ads where people dream of Egg McMuffins? Yeah, that's me. A gorgeous bright smile greets me as I pull up to the drive thru. It's on a face much younger than mine. He flirts with me every day and every day I flirt back. I'm in my early forties and a guy barely twenty is flirting with me!! I listen to music I used to listen to so that thoughts of him *(of having sex with him)* linger throughout my day. As the months go by, we get on friendlier terms until one day he is gone. He has probably moved on in his career or possibly gone back to school. I hadn't realized how much I missed the feeling of desire, the longing for someone else. I had also missed my chance. I had been led into temptation and God had led temptation away from me.

This feels like a dangerous place to be, here on the edge of darkness again. As I read through my past journals, trying to avoid nostalgia and regret, something else began to subtly creep in—a longing to go back. I found a drawing from someone in my past, someone who had been interested in me, but I didn't return the interest enough to date him. I was attracted to him, but I wasn't ready to jump back into a relationship that I had to be so invested in. I smile when I recall his face in my mind, his was a love I never had the opportunity to taint. It is an innocent enough train of thought . . . until it isn't. I start searching for him on social media, wanting to reconnect with this flicker of a flame that hasn't surfaced for over twenty years. The desire became a distraction.

How do I stop the spiral before it goes too far? How do I turn back to God as quick as I spin toward the shadows? I think of sin as being tangible like sex, but there are other ways we can become separated. I knew writing this book would become a part of my spiritual growth. I thought I was mature enough of a Christian to not get swallowed up by the hissing of the snake but hiss it did. And turn I did.

Doubt

Since I had walked away once, how easy would it be for me to walk away again?

Uncertainty eats away at me. I pray every hour on the hour, but I'm not getting the answer I expect. I continue to wait, hearing a voice trying to reassure me that he will stay true to what he has promised. Where is this doubt coming from then? I am listening to the wrong voice; I know this because God doesn't cause doubt. Am I slipping away? Crawling back to the night which entices me so? Someone is standing there in the shadows waiting for me to turn back around. He lurks around every corner of every street I turn down. He knows all my secrets.

I still hear the hissing of the snake, reminding me of the things I left behind:

Are you really buying into this? You haven't really changed at all. Do you see how you will fail? These words will go nowhere but in a trunk like all the rest.
God will not protect you. He will not be good to you.

The more I listen, the more I doubt. I can't do this; I can't write this book. I will disappoint God. The thought of failing God was almost reason enough to not continue down this road, but I had disappointed him so much already and yet he still took me back in open arms. Am I still waiting on God or am I the one causing the delay? Why is this taking so long, isn't it already too late? I say I will leave my worry at his feet, yet I pick it back up and take it back from him. I am the one who lacks faith God does not lack his promises. One day I will be grateful for the wait, grateful for the stillness of my days.

Then I hear the other voice, the only one I should be listening to:

Be proud of how far you have already come.
Don't keep looking back at the boat you stepped out of.
Don't roam around in a wilderness you were never meant to be in.

Fear

What happens when the shadows of your life creep up on you?

I run back into the shadows; I want to hide. There are things I still wanted to keep from God as if to say; "you can have all of me…except this." This piece of me that makes me feel like "me". Listening to certain music immerses me into my past self, the hard heart, the wall, the familiar protection. I still want to flirt with the darkness, I still want to walk too close to the edge. I let the darkness inspire me more than the light. The shadow is still my hiding place, my comfort zone. When am I going to let Jesus become the one I run to, the place I hide?

As March 2020 was putting the brakes on rush hour traffic, God was putting the brakes on me. God was forcing me to face parts of my life I hadn't in a long time. I still held personal relationships at bay preferring not to be vulnerable. I refused to put my heart on the line again and God was asking me to do just that. It wasn't about a man; it was about trusting God in an area where I didn't trust myself. I wanted to fast forward to my God-given purpose, the specific assignment he had for me. I knew it had to do with my passion for writing, but I didn't have the details I needed to proceed yet. What would I write about and where would the words go after they left me?

I worry that life is going to come crashing down on me. That this "up" will inevitably come down, that this Christian life won't work out for one reason or another. What do you call that kind of faith? *Lacking.* Believing God will only take me halfway OR I might do something to ruin it. Can I trust God to steer me the right way? I admit I am afraid to ask God to for anything. I don't believe he will do it either the way I want, or in a good way. Like if I ask him to help me lose weight and I get the stomach flu. Or asking for a dream you have had only to have it create more stress. Why do we doubt that God wants to be good to us? Maybe we think, we will eventually have to pay for our sins in some way.

I am inexplicably more afraid now than I was when I was roaming around as a prodigal. Perhaps it is because I am older and have stared grief in the face. I know how much it hurts. Each time I get in the car I say a silent prayer; "protect me from . . . an accident, a breakdown, a deer running across the road...someone intent on violence, a deadly virus." I am afraid I will die before I finish this book. Left undone it will remain on my laptop, password unknown. I will die before my dream is fulfilled. I worry when I know I shouldn't, that I should be at peace even though there is fear inside. Fear that also reveals my lack of faith. God will hold true to his promises, he is the only one who does.

"Stop looking back over your shoulder, anticipating the same disappointments that were there before. Your life has changed, you've changed." ~ God

Discipline

For God has not given us a spirit of fear and timidity,
but of power, love, and self-discipline.

—*2 Tim 1:7 NLT*

This wasn't the wilderness, it wasn't even the desert, I wasn't quite in "Mt Carmel" yet, so where am I? Had I hidden away in a cave? I feel like I need to ask for forgiveness, but for what exactly? I can't identify what this is, I just know it doesn't feel good. Do I have a desire to go back there to my prodigal years?

While writing this book, there were times when God was silent. I hadn't experienced his silence before and had assured myself that I wouldn't. I had done what God had asked, why would he be silent toward me? Why would he look away when I looked for him? Is this the place where faith resides? Confused, I turned back to what I knew, I looked back to Dallas—worship music and prayer. Maybe God wasn't the one being silent, maybe it was me. Trying to hide my thoughts, the desires that had crept in. When I realized I didn't want God to interrupt these thoughts of mine, that's when they became a sin.

You might think that once you are standing on solid ground that an earthquake will not cause a tremble. Think again . . . the snake is constantly fighting for your soul. Whether you have strayed or been faithful in your journey since you were ten, satan doesn't want you to win. Since I had spent so much time doing his will and serving on his side and I did it so well, he wanted me back. He likes the story I was writing before, not this one.

I have heard it said that "you must be doing something right if the devil is putting up such a fight". The darkness still calls to me, but I have already walked too far down this road. I have already given myself, my life, over to God and I can't go back now.

When I started writing this book, I was expecting a fight, so I had not been prepared for a more subtle approach from the snake. I wasn't ready for a surprise attack. I convinced myself it wasn't a slippery slope; "There's nothing wrong with remembering, nothing wrong with desire. Look up that old flame just to see what happen to him. *Wouldn't it be fun to do it again?*" Because it had been fun (albeit reckless) the first time around. I didn't just read about my past, I wanted to linger there. I started slipping further away from the surface, down to the nasty stuff that dwells at the bottom. Food for fish. There was Jesus standing on the water, his face shimmering, hand out to pull me back up—reminding me who I belonged to now. Not the dank dark ocean bottom surrounded by remnants of shipwrecks. I belong on the surface in the light with him.

*I ate no choice food; no meat or wine touched my lips;
and I used no lotions at all until the three weeks were over.*

—Dan 10:3 NIV

*Fasting detaches you from this world.
Prayer reattaches you to the next world.*

—Archbishop Fulton J. Sheen

14

Is Eating a Donut a Sin?

(Thoughts from a 21-day Fast)

January 6th, 2020

IT IS DAY ONE of my 21-day fast. I have never done this before, and I'm not convinced I will succeed. Everyone who knows me on a personal level, including Jesus, knows I'm not a pleasant person before breakfast. As such, I compromise and keep breakfast as is. For the rest of the day, I will eat only fruits and vegetables. I am calling it a "partial Daniel-fast". I will give up a few of my routine comforts. I will switch secular music for worship, and instead of listening to audiobooks I will go for more intentional prayer time. I have purchased the book "Pursuit" by Dave Patterson, to guide me along and to record my thoughts.

I start with a shopping spree to my favorite market. I load up on fruits, plant-based burgers, and (yikes!) tofu. By the end of my workday, I am stuffed having overcompensated to hold off hunger pangs. Note to self: eat less tomorrow.

I pray three times bowing low on the floor of my office, facing east. I pray for my sisters' broken hearts, for a bad accident which has occurred on the Pennsylvania turnpike, the wildfires in Australia, and for the people at the border. I pray for God to provide clarity for my purpose and to bless my upcoming trip to Israel.

I don't think I will make it through. I'm pretty sure I will give in. I hope I make it.

January 7th, 2020

It's an ordinary Tuesday that doesn't feel ordinary. I stay on track with the veggies, fruits, and devoted prayer time. I am upbeat, feeling blessed simply just by making the decision to participate in this fast.

I had a dream last night: I am standing in the grass beside train tracks. A locomotive is whizzing by but slows down enough for me to see Jesus reaching his arm out of a window. He is inviting me to put my hand in his and he says, *"Come on, get in, you're ready."*

January 9th, 2020

I have made it through the first week and I don't feel like doing this anymore. I'm not really sacrificing anything so what is this even about?

January 10th, 2020

I am listless today. I stay on track with my fast and prayer time but with far less passion then when I began.

January 12th, 2020

I am sitting in a class at church to determine my spiritual gifts. I'm not entirely comfortable and am distracted as old church hang-ups start to haunt me. I am finding all the reasons to not commit. I stay seated and wearily participate. I am so unenthused about this, and I am started to get perturbed. *Why are all the teachers men?*

A Light in the Darkness

January 13th, 2020

Tonight, my church is having a special prayer service. I am tired from work and almost decide not to go. We stand in a circle on stage praying together then go to individual seats to pray by ourselves. I say an unexpected prayer and leave grateful I made the choice to come.

January 15th, 2020

One of my co-workers has brought in Timbits. I don't even try to resist—I take two. *Is eating a donut a sin?* I expect to feel guilty, but I don't. I go to the basement during my lunch hour to walk on the treadmill. Instead, I kneel on the concrete floor and pray with a renewed fervor. Back in my office, I get a call from the church asking me to be a greeter. God has opened a door to serve.

January 16th, 2020

On my way home from work, I stop at a Kroger. When I walk in, they are handing out samples of butternut squash pretzels. *Sounds like plant-based to me!* God has given me a snack.

January 17th, 2020

I am starting to fade. I give in and run to my old comforts—listening to music I haven't listened to in a long time. It's hard hip-hop music which takes me back to my old self, back to sinful memories. *Why am I still running to old comforts instead of God?*

January 19th, 2020

I haven't received the clarity I was expecting about my purpose. A Christian production company has gotten my name from a client and asks me to produce a poster for an upcoming concert. God has given me a new client.

Is Eating a Donut a Sin?

January 20th, 2020

I search for some new Christian music to listen to and discover hip-hop Christian artists like J Moss and Anthony Brown. Now I can listen to my favorite kind of music and worship! God has given me a playlist.

January 21st, 2020

Jesus goes for the jugular. I sense him asking me to trust him with something I can't trust myself with. I have sworn off men and falling in love again. Yet, I sense some feelings starting to develop for someone. This is an old pattern of mine, and I am anxious.

January 23rd, 2020

Jesus is frustrating me, and I just want a steak!

January 24th, 2020

The fast is coming to an end and I am disappointed it's almost over. *How can I keep this intimacy with God when I return to my normal eating habits?*

January 26th, 2020

It's the last day of the fast. Was it successful? Well . . . I slipped up some. But at some point, during the past 21-days, it became less about what I was eating and more about being devoted to God. I was listening to him more. My prayers increased and were more intentional. I received some unexpected opportunities to serve. By pursuing him exclusively I stopped wasting my time being focused on other things. It took my relationship with God to the next level. *Why doesn't this slice of pizza taste as good as it used to?*

Yahweh,
Look how you have changed me!
Search my heart
my speech is stuck
In the way you choke me up—
The love you have bestowed upon
your daughter,
your beloved,
Yours.

15

The Light of my Life

*... whoever follows me will never walk in darkness but will
have the light of life.*

—*John 8:12 NIV*

ALL MY LIFE, I couldn't forget it—couldn't erase those hours spent
in that little white church and all those times my parents forced me
to go. I learned about Jesus from day one of my life. Now I think,
wasn't I one of the lucky ones?

Sun drenched; I am walking around the neighborhood talking to Jesus like I did during the early days of my return. With a
sudden burst of energy, I start to jog. God is asking me to take
yet another leap of faith, to leave behind the nine to five and start
living the writing life I had always dreamed of. I have walked many
miles with Jesus, now it was time to run with him.

The more I talk to God and dig into his words, the hungrier
I become for him. My passion built up for the Bible I had once
thrown away, for this life I had once thrown away. I can remember
the way I felt before, in my early adulthood when I walked away
from God. I desperately wanted to reject how I had been raised.

Now I recall my teenage Christianity with fondness. I listen to songs I used to own on cassettes and read through the song lyrics I wrote expressing my young love for God.

There are days when my gaze drifts away. When my head hits my pillow, there is a gnawing sense of something I forgot to do. I *miss* Jesus when I don't spend time with him. My former self does not recognize this new me. The relationship I spent twenty years tearing apart has been fully restored in the few years I have been back. There is no fence left to straddle.

I have always been envious of people's love stories. People who met their spouses in high school and are still married almost thirty years later. People who met once, missed their chance, then meet again years later. I have learned to enjoy my single life, to thrive in it even. Relationships always seemed to weigh me down. I have not been lucky in love . . . or so I thought. I dreamed of someone who would go to the ends of the earth for me. Someone who would chase me when my pride, bitterness, or restlessness caused me to run away. Someone who loved me enough to die for me. The funny thing is, I had that someone and I never knew it. Picture someone who has been separated from the love of their life for a long time, watch the way they run into each other's arms when they see each other again. That is what it felt like when I returned to Jesus after decades of being separated from him.

And so, this has become *my* beautiful love story.

I found the lily in my valley
I found strength when I was worn
I found a place to leave my burdens;
I found refuge from the storm.
A place where I trade my dark skies
for beaming rays of sunshine
I found the lily in my valley
And He blooms all the time.

— Quinton Mills, "I Found the Lily in my Valley"

16

Dawn

Then your light will break out like the dawn,
and your recovery will speedily spring forth . . .

—*Isa 58:8 NASB*

So, we have the prophetic word made more sure, to which
you do well to pay attention as to a lamp shining in a dark
place, until the day dawns and the morning star arises in your
hearts.

—*2 Pet 1:19 NASB*

It is a brilliant blue-sky day in early October 2021. I have just taken a walk through Dawes Arboretum and am on my way home. Eighties music is coming through my speakers. I am steeped in nostalgia with a big grin on my face. It is a "day off" from writing this book and I am soaking in this beautiful autumn day. Reading through my old journals has brought back a flood of memories and some surprises. I found a picture a guy had drawn for me over twenty-five years ago. We hadn't been romantically involved. I don't know why I kept it; I don't know why it survived the Dallas purge but there it was after all these years. I remember the way his black hair flopped over to one side when he smiled down on me, and I smile at the memory. This perfectly safe, innocent memory would become a distraction.

The subtle hiss would become a conversation. Satan started fighting me for this book. He didn't use the bad memories—he used the good ones to deter me. I started looking for my old friend on social media, started texting phone numbers to see if one of them would be him. The search only lasted a few days and the desire diminished quickly. That was just the beginning of the snake coiling around this book.

I began to feel inexplicably separated from God. As if my relationship with him was dependent upon writing this book. I was treating it as if it were something I was checking off my to-do list. I had lost my passion for it.

One day my phone rang, and I looked down to see I was getting a call from Carrollton, Texas. *Dallas was calling.* A guy named Jonathan from Covenant Church asked me if I had anything I wanted him to pray over me for. I hesitantly started to tell him about leaving my job and writing this book. As he prayed, I was enveloped with peace. God had used Dallas once again to affirm the direction he was leading me.

It took a lot of praying and faith to continue to put this book together on those days where I didn't feel as if these words would go anywhere. And if they did, that they would matter to anyone aside from myself. Finally, I gave the book, my dream, back to God. It could go where he wanted it to go. I can't dream bigger than God, so I started trusting him. My passion was renewed, and the words started to flow again.

When I think of the peace living inside of me, that I can't understand or explain, I am overwhelmed. I returned to where I belonged all along. I returned the creation back over to its creator. We belong to him; we are children of the day. When we choose to walk away, we leave behind the peace he wants us to have. We leave behind that abundant life he intends for us.

It takes the armor of God to fight the darkness. It takes resistance, faith, and listening to God's voice. We carry our scars; both the ones we cause, and the ones caused by others. Our past decisions come back to haunt us in many ways; that person we said goodbye to that we now regret not holding on to, those selfish acts and their cost, the many things we say and do over a lifetime. It's amazing to think of what we are spared because of Jesus, and all that has been forgiven.

I'm not sure where you stand in your relationship with God or if you have ever had one; if you are currently straddling the fence or if you are a wandering prodigal. Whoever you are, wherever your faith currently stands, I implore you to come home.

Your Father is waiting.

Recommended Playlist

"Come Alive (Dry Bones)", Lauren Daigle
"When God Ran", Benny Hester
"Candle in the Rain", David Meece
"Learning to Trust", David Meece
"The Lily in my Valley", Quinton Mills
"Reckless Love", Cory Asbury
"Rattle", Elevation Worship
"Graves into Gardens", Elevation Worship
"Testify to Love", Avalon
"King of my Heart", Kutless

Recommended Reading

"Don't Settle for Safe", Sarah Jakes Roberts
"The Dream of You", Jo Saxton
"Jesus Feminist", Sarah Bessey
"Whisper", Mark Batterson
"Planted with a Purpose", TD Jakes
"Dangerous Prayers", Craig Groeschel